Fancy's Way

by

James J. Adams

Order this book online at www.trafford.com
or email orders@trafford.com

Most Trafford titles are also available at major online book retailers.

Note for Librarians: A cataloguing record for this book is available from Library
and Archives Canada at www.collectionscanada.ca/amicus/index-e.html

Printed in Victoria, BC, Canada.

ISBN: 978-1-4269-1321-1 (sc)

*We at Trafford believe that it is the responsibility of us all, as both individuals and corporations,
to make choices that are environmentally and socially sound. You, in turn, are supporting this
responsible conduct each time you purchase a Trafford book, or make use of our publishing services.
To find out how you are helping, please visit www.trafford.com/responsiblepublishing.html*

*Our mission is to efficiently provide the world's finest, most comprehensive book publishing
service, enabling every author to experience success. To find out how to publish your book, your
way, and have it available worldwide, visit us online at www.trafford.com*

Trafford rev. 6/25/2009

 www.trafford.com

North America & international
toll-free: 1 888 232 4444 (USA & Canada)
phone: 250 383 6864 ♦ fax: 250 383 6804 ♦ email: info@trafford.com

The United Kingdom & Europe
phone: +44 (0)1865 487 395 ♦ local rate: 0845 230 9601
facsimile: +44 (0)1865 481 507 ♦ email: info.uk@trafford.com

CHAPTER 1

"*I* am not having any more children. Lord, help me if I have to bring any more children into this world. This is the last one and it better be a girl." Those were the excited words of Mrs. Pearl as she prepared to give birth for the fifth time. This baby was a girl. Ms. Fancy was born during a period of National chaos. She was born in the summer of 1964, right in the midst of the struggle for Civil Rights. The season was hot and so were the emotions of Fancy's fellow Mississippians. But, the hot tempers of the day were not relegated to the Southern States, the entire nation was on alert. Because of the social climate surrounding Fancy's birth, the midwife, Ms. Eula slapped the baby on the butt, held her up high so the Lord could get a good view and she promptly named the pretty Black baby, Fancy. Fancy did not cry like this was her first appearance in the world. No, this child cried like she had some living experience. To borrow from the old cliché, the baby girl cried like she'd been here before. Fancy's mother, Mrs. Pearl Debonair had to ask the midwife why she thought Fancy would be a suitable name for her only girl child? Remember, this is 1964 which history records as a period of

Black pride. Brother James Brown sang his hit tune, "Say it loud, I am Black and I'm proud." Mrs. Pearl desired a distinctive sounding name befitting a princess, a name that would make her child standout from the crowded field of pretty Black girls. She further reasoned that her baby should have a name that would gain the attention of descent, aspiring and honorable young Black men and a name that would hopefully open some doors for her daughter. Fancy's mama had no idea of the greatness, the drama, the disappointment and triumphs that awaited her baby girl. After staring Fancy over one last time, Ms. Eula stood her ground and stated with authority, as if to say to Fancy's mama not to question her, "this child had it" and more. The child would be blessed by God himself. Not only would she touch and influence the lives of others, her personal example would help others as they sought to change their lives. Everything that the baby girl would do in her life would give her admirers and her enemies the impression that she was trying to be fancy." Even her suffering and setbacks would give others the idea that Fancy had an easy life. However, dealing with adversity and loss in a dignified manner would be one of Fancy's greatest strengths. The midwife ended the name debate and the name Fancy W. Debonair was official and ready for printing on the child's birth certificate and business cards. The W was for Wilma. Mrs. Pearl insisted on her child's middle name being after her great grandmother. The midwife slowly and gently handed Fancy to her happy mama who was still lying in the darkened spare bedroom of her family's home. Fancy's mama smiled brightly. Then she told the midwife that her husband would pay her the day after tomorrow. The midwife was glad to hear this. She didn't mind helping the family, but she wanted her money. Otis Debonair Jr., Fancy's father entered the bedroom at the same moment Ms. Eula prepared to leave. As Ms. Eula exited the room, she smiled at Mr. Debonair as if she knew something that he did not. He had seen that smile before and realized that his wife had reassured Ms. Eula regarding her payment. Mr. Debonair entered the bedroom and closed the door, leaving enough crack in it to allow a touch of light. He then eased over anxiously to take a peek at their baby girl. Mrs. Pearl handed him the child and told him her name was Ms. Fancy Wilma Debonair. Otis Jr. grabbed Fancy and held her in his mechanics hands. His hands and the child became one. He rubbed the child's forehead and her face gently and repeatedly. Unlike his wife, Otis Debonair accepted the baby's name immediately. He thought Fancy added to Wilma was like a simple math problem. Fancy is a new name, combined with an old name like Wilma equaled a child of destiny. He said, "Yeah, she looks like a Fancy." His wife rolled her eyes and thought to herself, how would he know what a Fancy looked like? Shortly, Fancy's four older brothers made their way into the small room, a room that did not have central air conditioning. Additional bodies in the bedroom meant more competition for the little cool air that was already struggling to satisfy Otis Jr., Mrs. Pearl and Fancy. There was an electric fan in the room which sat about six feet away from Mrs. Debonair. The fan was missing a blade and it was working as hard as it could, but the desired cooling results were minimal. To fight the evening heat, there was also a collection of handheld paper fans. You remember the fans that they used to pass out in Church. Anyway, Fancy's brothers were excited to meet their sister. When Jeremiah, the youngest of Fancy's brothers got a close examination of her, he said that it did not matter that she was a girl. He was going to teach her how to play football. Jeremiah really anticipated dumping some of his chores on Fancy so he'd have more time to sneak off and play with his boyfriends. The other three brothers, the oldest being Blackmon, after Blackmon came Will, then Stare; they did not share in Jeremiah's plan. They intended to protect their sister with everything available to them. After their brief introduction to their sister, Otis Jr. asked the boys to leave the room. Jeremiah quickly asked if he could go out and play. His father told him to go play with his school books. The family had worked hard to instill in their children that school work always came before playing marbles and hanging out with the no good children in the neighborhood. Mr. Debonair asked Blackmon to make sure that his brothers engaged their studies and to make especially sure that Jeremiah went over his reading assignment. Jeremiah was reading at the average grade level, but his father did not think the boy was at an acceptable standard and stayed on the boy to improve. Mr. and Mrs. Pearl Debonair spent a few extra minutes in the room with their baby. They held hands and said a prayer – a prayer full of thankfulness. They were thankful that their child was born healthy and with functioning limbs. At that moment though, as the child let out a good cry, they realized that her lungs and voice box were working exceptionally well too. Otis Jr. was thankful that his wife had delivered the baby without any problems of her own. She would be off her feet for a couple of days to recover. Her mother-in-law, who lived a few blocks over was warned that she'd have to change her weekly schedule to help the family. After their prayer, they contemplated the future of their child. Obviously, they were not novices to the daddy and mama roles. They were experienced enough to know that raising a little Black girl would be different than raising little Black boys. Otis Jr. remembered out loud how his father had to protect his sisters from all sorts of men who wanted nothing more than to spoil their package. Otis Jr. was the only boy in his family of six. He reflected on how his father kept the girls on a tight leash. Otis Jr. and Mrs. Pearl were hopeful that the world had changed enough where they would not have to be overbearing in trying raise and protect their daughter. Mr. Debonair joked about retrieving his father's old pistol from underneath the wood floor. He kept the pistol in the wannabe master bedroom where he and his wife slept. The pistol was located underneath the wood floor, on his side of the bed, wrapped in a torn burlap bag to shield it from nosy insects and dust. Otis Jr.'s father gave him the pistol as part of his last will and testament. His father did not have much to give him. But, his father made certain that his only man child inherited the pistol that was more for show than anything else. The reading of his father's will was a very emotional and near traumatic ordeal for Otis Jr. Growing up, Otis Jr. had known his father as a strong and sharing family man. His father wasn't perfect by any means. But, the man was his rock and his untimely death due to pancreatic cancer was a shock and emotional drain. When his father was diagnosed with cancer, the disease was well beyond the stage where treatment could help. Otis Jr. and Pearl named their second Will in memory of Otis' father's strength and resolve. Like his grandfather, Will had to fight for his life. Will's birth was troubling, the family wasn't sure if he'd live through the night. Ms. Eula also delivered Will. She stayed with Will the entire night of his birth. She was determined that the boy would live and hid did. In this day and time, she would not be called a midwife; she'd probably be called a surrogate mother. So, the family had plenty to be thankful about. Otis Jr. teased with the idea of taking Fancy in public. Before every public outing, he would place that old pistol in the front of his trousers, with the pistol's handle polished brightly, making it clearly visible for the daredevils to see. His wife patted him on the shoulder and told him that the pistol would not be necessary. Besides, they both knew that old pistol didn't even have a firing pin. Otis Jr. kept the firing pin in a different location from the pistol. He did that in case one of the boys happened to find it. Mr. Debonair looked forward to riding through town with his boys and Fancy in his red 1958 Buick. Taking his children for a joy ride in the car was one of the simple pleasures that the whole family had learned to appreciate. The rides were like family dinners. By the end of each ride, all of the boys arrived back home asleep and ready for bed. You know how it is when you take a flight somewhere and when the plane lands at your destination, the flight stewardess will announce over the planes' public address system, welcome to this town? And, she makes her announcement as if she's the designated spokesperson or one woman welcoming committee for that city. Well, Fancy Wilma Debonair was welcomed to little Mississippi and the big world by everyone except her paternal grandmother, Ms. Hattimae Debonair.

Price of change

Change

Change is like the price of electricity,

bread, milk and gas

Change

The price never stays the same

It rises rapidly - it declines just as fast

Change

One thing for certain

Change will always have a price

CHAPTER 2

Three whole days had sneaked by since Fancy W. Debonair had joined her family and fellow Mississippians. And, still her paternal grandma, Ms. Hattimae had not made her way over to lay eyes on or hold the child in her own arms. During her own youth, Grandma Debonair used her arms used to cradle wet and sticky tobacco leafs as well as baskets full of freshly plucked cotton. It wasn't as if Ms. Hattimae did not know of Fancy's birth. Of course, Ms. Hattimae had heard the news of Fancy's birth from everyone in town, especially from the extremely talkative Ms. Eula, who was known as one to share gossip even before that gossip had a chance to leave someone else's mouth. Fancy's family started to wonder what was taking Ms. Hattimae so long to visit the family. After all, Ms. Hattimae was on the scene within twenty-four hours for the births of her grandsons. As they say, she was in the house; In the house helping the family with meals, running errands and keeping the older children focused on their priorities. Ms. Hattimae would gladly forsake her normal activities to help her son's family. Besides, the two and three nights of weekly Church activities were getting to be too expensive for her pocketbook. According to her, attending Church was no longer about the Word of God or preparing sinner souls to enter heaven. These days, it was about the all mighty dollar. She lived on a budget and she figured the Lord just had to understand and forgive her for keeping a little to pay her bills. But, since the passing of her husband seven years earlier, Church was the one social activity that she used to occupy her free time. Ms. Hattimae had a history and a story. Folks in town did not know much about her personal life and they dared to get in her business. She did not play that game. She liked to describe herself as a dignified lady. On Sunday morning, just as the first offering plate was being passed around at her Church, Grandma Debonair knocked on the door of her son's home. Otis Jr. offered to pick her up and give her a ride. But, she only lived three blocks over on South 1st Street, so she walked over. Everything that she needed was within a short walking distance of her home and she didn't mind walking. As she arrived at her son's house, she wasn't exactly wearing her Sunday best. However, she was dressed quite nattily. Starting with her prune colored foot wear, which had a striped bow stapled across the top. She loved prunes and anything adorned in the color of prunes. Her foot problem meant she could not risk wearing sharp heels, so her shoes had heels that were an inch and a half high with extra wide soles. She also had on knee highs which were slightly lighter in color than her shoes. Her dress itself wasn't the typical "old lady" dress. It was a cream flavor, almost like Butter Pecan, it dropped maybe four inches below her knees and it still fit the way it did ten years earlier. To top off her outfit, she had a purse that she bought from the nickel and dime store. The purse looked a little aged, but she polished it up and it matched her shoes perfectly. Lastly, she had on a flowered sun hat to protect her hairdo from the summer breeze. You might get the impression that Grandma spent her few funds on clothing, but you'd be dead wrong. The woman just knew how to make her clothes last and she knew how to get the most out of what little she did have. As she lifted her hand to knock on the door a second time, her oldest grandson, Blackmon moved to shout, "Who is it?" After hearing his Grandma respond in her usual commanding voice, he shouted through the house that Grandma was at the door. With that, he opened the door. Ms. Hattimae entered the home; she suspended her judgment of the home's current interior condition. The home was not clean to her standard, but she certainly understood why. The family spent the last three days catering and adjusting to Fancy's arrival. She made her way in the house, dodging and stepping over hand-me-down toys. The family did not have the money or disposable income to celebrate Christmas in the traditional way. Otis Jr. came from the back of the home to greet his mother. She removed her hat and handed it to Blackmon to place in a space where it would not be bothered by anyone except her. She then lowered her pocketbook from her right shoulder for Blackmon to hide it in the same secret space. Blackmon knew exactly where to hide his Grandma's belongings. He and Grandma had long ago agreed upon that space; the two of them had what you would call a 'special arrangement.' Otis Jr. shared a tight embrace with his mother. Jeremiah, Will and Stare waited in line to get their hugs from their Grandma. The boys were happy to see Grandma because she knew how to cook their favorites. Every since their mom gave birth, the boys took it as punishment for having to eat the meals that their father referred to as food fit for young boys who wanted to be strong like their daddy. As Otis Jr. embraced his mom, he whispered that he needed to speak with her privately before she started in the kitchen. She agreed to have the conversation wither son, but she did not look forward to the conversation because she knew that her son wanted to pry into her business. She knew what her son wanted to discuss and she was prepared to tell him what she always told him. Also, she realized that her son was exercising his duty as a son in attempting to look out for his mother. While he could not prove it, Otis Jr. suspected that his mother was being courted by a male 'friend'. No matter how Otis Jr. tried to find out if this were indeed a fact or rumor, he could not get any information. His mother was a discreet woman, respectable and all that jazz. The neighborhood gossip channels didn't even know what Grandma Debonair was up to. As far as she was concerned, whatever she did, how she did and who she did it with was her business. Well, it was her business and the Lord's business. Her son though, was on the hunt for her mystery 'man friend.' After embracing her son, Grandma Debonair moved down the line to embrace her grandsons in the order that they were lined up. After all of the hugs, Otis Jr. escorted his mother to the back room so she could meet his only daughter. Ms. Fancy was lying fast asleep when her Grandma walked in to meet her. Before picking up the resting baby, Grandma Debonair stood over the child taking in and appreciating the miracle that is called life. She picked up Ms. Fancy and the baby let out a small cry. Fancy's cry was sharp but short. As her Grandma held her, Fancy resorted to kicking her legs and expressing in baby language that she did not appreciate being bothered, especially when she was in the middle of a good nap. The spirits of Ms. Hattimae and Fancy locked onto one another. Fancy wasn't afraid of her new acquaintance. Grandma Debonair held her grandbaby at arms distance so she could look in the child's eyes. Grandma Debonair must have seen something in Fancy's eyes. Grandma Debonair whispered, "Oh, my Jesus." She held Fancy safely and pulled the child to her bosom. Grandma Debonair reflected on every detail that Ms. Eula told her about Fancy. Because of the Ms. Eula's permanent affair with gossip and untruths, Grandma Debonair could only believe half of what the midwife told her about anything. However, Grandma Debonair agreed that every word from Ms. Eula's mouth was right on target about Fancy. But, she could not get herself to tell Ms Eula that she was right because Ms. Eula would never stop talking about how much she think knows about newborns. As she held the baby girl, Grandma Debonair repeated, "Oh my Jesus." Otis Jr. looked at his mother with a curios look, but Grandma Debonair did not feel obligated to share her reasons for repeatedly saying, "Oh my Jesus." But, what actually scared Grandma Debonair was how much she saw her younger self in the eyes and face Ms. Fancy. To escape the moment, Grandma Debonair started to think about the next week or so that she would spend taking care of the boys, tending to her daughter-in-law and Fancy. She placed the baby on the bed as she and her son left the room to have a conversation that he so desperately wanted to have with her. As the two of them entered the living room, the boys were seated at the kitchen table expecting their Grandma to start whipping up some real food. Otis Jr. was relieved that the boys were in the kitchen because that meant they were out of hearing distance for the conversation that he was about to have with his mother. Grandma Debonair noticed her grandsons seated at the table and gave them a teaser by reaching for and putting her cooking apron around her waist. With that movement, Grandma gave the boys a clue that good food was on the way, the boys just smiled with anticipation. Grandma Debonair's apron was a canvass of Gala apples, nectarines, pears and of course her favorite-prunes. She reached around her back to tie the apron in a tight knot and continued following her son into the living room. In the living room, Otis Jr. took the same seat that he would take when he was preparing to lecture one or all of the boys on an important issue. He expected his mother would also take a seat directly in front of him. But, his mother just stood, her mind was on preparing a delicious meal for her grandsons. She was also wondering how many trips to the store she and Blackmon would have to make for basic menu ingredients. But, before any of that could get started, she still had to poke her in head in the wannabe master bedroom and say hello to her daughter-in-law. Grandma Debonair stood half patiently in front of her son as she waited his inquiries. The moment was tense for Otis Jr., but his mother was as cool as a cold soda in the summer months. Then, her son asked, "Mama, what is going on?" Grandma Debonair was a pretty good card player in her youth. She knew that her son was getting around to asking about her male companion. But, she played along as though she had no idea what her son was up to. So, she asked in her most confused voice, "What do you mean by, "What is going on?" Her son replied, "Come on mama, you know what I mean." Grandma Debonair was now out of patience with her son's weak interrogation into her personal affairs. She was eager to get on with the purpose of her visit. She looked over her left shoulder at her grandsons as they waited with eating utensils in the ready position. So, her son mustered up his courage and finally asked her directly, "Mama, do you have a man friend, that is all I want to know." Grandma Debonair walked closer to her son and rubbed him on the head. She thanked him kindly for his concern and she whispered some other kind words to make him feel like he'd received the information that he was after. However, she did not deny that she had a male friend, nor did she say anything to confirm that she had a male friend. See, no one gets in the business of Grandma Debonair, not even her son. With that, she headed to the kitchen to break in the pots that she bought for son's family, the same pots that never got used by a good cook unless she was doing the cooking. At least, that's how she felt. As she walked off, her son just sat in his lecture seat thinking what he was going to do with his mother. He noticed a pattern though. His wife and his mother both rubbed his face, shoulder or head whenever they needed to get out of something. He was getting more rubs than he was getting answers to his questions. The conversation with his mama made him think about Ms. Fancy. He asked himself, "would Fancy have the same level of independence as his mama? Just thinking about that made him shake his head.

The Reality

The Dream

Remember your dream

Cherish it

Nourish your dream

The Reality

Reflect on your reality

Embrace it

Deal effectively with your realities

CHAPTER 3

Happy birthday to you, Happy Birthday to you, Happy Birthday - Ms. Fancy. The Debonair family gathered to celebrate Fancy's second birthday. For a two year old, she was already living up to her name. In the Debonair home, Fancy's family could not turn their backs on her for a moment. If they did turn their backs on Fancy, she would get into everything that was within her reach. It was Grandma Debonair's habit to bake the children a birthday cake and on this day, she made a special cake for Fancy. Even though Fancy had stolen Grandma Debonair's heart, Grandma Debonair made sure that she wasn't guilty of treating Fancy too better than she treated her brothers. It probably was the fact that Fancy was a little girl that caused Grandma Debonair to giver her a little extra. Grandma Debonair would not admit it publicly, but Fancy's birthday cake did have an extra layer of vanilla icing on it. Grandma Debonair and her male companion, Mr. Henry, arrived for the party about twenty minutes before Otis Jr. was expected to arrive home. Otis Jr. had not been able to find any information on his mama's male suitor. Little did he know that he would finally meet his mama's mystery man. He enlisted the help of his sisters, but they were in the dark as much as he was. Otis Jr. was so hard-up to know something about this gentleman that he stooped to the lowest of lows by asking Ms. Eula if she knew anything. Ms. Eula was upset more than she was surprised that there was something going on that she did not have the scoop on. So, rather than her admit defeat, Ms. Eula lied to Otis Jr. and claimed that she knew all about the guy, but she was sworn to secrecy. The twenty minute gap between Grandma Debonair and Mr. Henry's arrival and the expected time for her son to arrive home was more than enough time for her to have a little girl talk with her daughter-in-law. She introduced Mr. Henry to her daughter-in-law and grandchildren. During their introduction to Mr. Henry, the boys acted like distinguished gentlemen from the upper levels of society. In the old days, we would say that the boys have good manners. Their behavior was a sign that their mother and father were teaching them well. But, the teachings were not yet taking a hold of Fancy. She pounced around the kitchen and giggled as if she was aware that the whole day was about her. Grandma Debonair asked Mr. Henry to place the cake, candles and birthday presents on the kitchen table. He did so and then entertained the children while Grandma Debonair and her daughter-in-law moved off to the living room for a quick conversation. As the two women walked, Grandma Debonair inched ahead of her daughter-in-law so she could plop down in her son's lecture seat. The seat is also known as the seat of authority and power. Now, Grandma Debonair occupied the lecture seat. She wanted her daughter-in-law to focus her attention on what she was about to say. As her daughter-in-law prepared to sit down on the rickety corner of the family's sofa, Grandma Debonair started by saying, "Listen baby, see that handsome, brown man right there?" The younger Debonair woman shook her up and down to indicate that she did see the handsome man. As Mrs. Pearl shook her head up and down, she managed to mumble, "Yes Mam." Grandma Debonair continued, "He's sweet to me, he's good company, and he's kind. Are you listening to me baby? Grandma Debonair continued, "More importantly, what Mr. Henry and I do is our business. My son doesn't need to know anything about this. Are we clear?" Her daughter-in-law got the message. This was not the time to be asking Grandma Debonair any questions. So, she simply said, "Yes Mam." That was the end of the lecture as presented by Grandma Debonair. I imagine college students would love taking Grandma Deboair's courses because she keeps her lectures very short. The daughter-in-law knew that her mother-in-law could take care of herself and the old lady was a good judge of character. On top of that, Grandma Debonair had volunteered to take the boys to her house after the birthday party to spend the night. Fancy would be the lone child in the house and that meant some loving for Otis Jr. and his wife. Mrs. Pearl was not about to pry into Grandma Debonair's business and risk rubbing Grandma Debonair the wrong way. She and Otis Jr. were going to rush Ms. Fancy off to her bath and bed so the two of them could have some private and quality love time. To get Ms. Fancy to bed early though, they would have to limit her intake of sugary cake and juice. Otherwise, Ms. Fancy would bounce around all night. With five children to raise, Pearl Debonair recognized how difficult it was to get quality time with her husband. She vowed to keep her mouth closed concerning her conversation with Grandma Debonair. Grandma Debonair wondered to herself if her daughter-in-law could really keep her mouth closed. But, she had to trust Mrs. Pearl. Grandma Debonair had no real reason for keeping her son out of her affairs other than she liked to keep her business to herself and she shared it with as few people as possible and then at the time of her choosing. The two women headed back to the kitchen. Shortly thereafter, Otis Jr. arrived home from the garage. Grandma Debonair introduced Mr. Henry to her son as simply, "a friend." Friend, her son thought to himself. I bet this is the character who's sweet on my mother. Mr. Henry was just like Grandma Debonair, he was a quiet man of very few words. After Fancy's birthday bash, Grandma Debonair packed up the boys and their overnight bags. She, Mr. Henry and the boys headed out the door. Otis Jr. was sure that his mother had told his wife something about Mr. Henry. Maybe what she told his wife was minimal, but it was something he was determined to find out. As planned, the two of them bathed Fancy and speeded her to bed. Otis Jr. thought he would please his wife, satisfy her and she'd spill her guts on Mr. Henry. Well, he satisfied his wife. He made all kinds of funny sounds, he groaned, grabbed, he pulled and then they rested. Mrs. Pearl placed her sweaty face on his chest. In a twist, Otis Jr. figured he'd try to rub his wife the way that she sometimes rubbed him whenever she wanted something. Then, as if he would no doubt get an honest answer, he asked his wife if his mother had said anything about that fella, Mr. Henry? His wife, knowing what her husband was up to and knowing that if she told what she knew, it would be a long time before Grandma Debonair afforded her a night like this one, responded, "Honey, your mother did not say a word to me about Mr. Henry." Usually, Otis Jr. would have pressed his wife for information, but he knew better than to do that. It was more important to spend the night away in love. So, they loved.

The world has needs

The world has needs

The worlds needs something to feel good about

A reason to restore its confidence

The Believers would say the world has Jesus and Faith

He's all that the world needs to feel good about

The people have needs

Something rather than money, material and doubt

CHAPTER 4

The telephone at the Debonair home rang, it rang like something was wrong. Old folks had the belief that they could tell when something tragic happened because of the way the telephone rang. If the telephone rang at three o'clock in the morning, then for sure, something was wrong. However, in the case of the Debonair's, there telephone was ringing in the middle of the weekday. The only telephone in the home was located on the north kitchen wall, just next to the white refrigerator. The silver handle of the refrigerator used to have four screws to keep it attached to the door. Now, between her growing boys constantly opening the refrigerator door as they searched for snacks and Otis Jr. pulling on the handle like one would an old fashioned slot machine; Mrs. Debonair's refrigerator handle was missing a screw and a half. Yeah, Otis Jr. did his best to fix the darn thing every time it broke, but the repair job did not last very long. Hungry children don't know how to pull lightly on the doors that stand between them and eating. Whenever most of the family was away from home, hearing the telephone was a concern for anyone in the backroom of the house. On this midday, that is precisely where Mrs. Debonair and Fancy were located as they finished reviewing Ms. Fancy's studies and prepared for her nap. Fancy wasn't quite demonstrating the joy of learning like her brothers. But, she enjoyed asking her grandma about girl stuff. When Otis Jr. wasn't home, Grandma would allow Fancy to dress up like a little five year old lady. On the other hand, the single telephone was in a good location because it reminded Mrs. Debonair how often she needed to remove all of the contents from the refrigerator and unplug it so the built up ice could thaw. After the iced thawed, she had to clean up the melted water and put the food back in the refrigerator before any of it had a chance to spoil. As Mrs. Debonair made a pallet on the bedroom floor for Fancy to take her nap, her mind on was preparing dinner. The pallet where Fancy lay to take her nap was made by Mrs. Debonair's deceased mother. The quilts were made from old clothes and extra material that Mrs. Debonair's mother refused to throw away. Some patches in the quilts were made from old blue jeans, shirts filled with washed sweat from field workers and just about any cloth that Mrs. Debonair's mother could get her hands on. Before she started for the kitchen, Mrs. Pearl made sure Fancy's eyes were fighting sleep. Mrs. Pearl reached over to turn the radio on, she was sure the music would cause Fancy to lose her battle with the nap that was calling her name. The telephone continued ringing. Mrs. Pearl Debonair had just turned to leave Fancy in the bedroom. She finally had an opportunity to break away from Ms. Fancy. Mrs. Pearl must have the same instincts as the old folks. As she raced to the telephone, she thought that something wasn't right. She quickened her step to get to the telephone. It's not as if she had a terribly long walk from the room where Fancy was napping to the kitchen. The family lived in a twelve-hundred square foot house with three bedrooms. There was no formal dining, greenhouse, tea room, gym formal living, library, den or laundry room. But, in that short walk; Mrs. Pearl mind ran crazy with something is wrong situations. Her first thought was maybe Otis Jr. had an accident in the garage. Otis Jr. had a habit of calling his wife whenever something went wrong in the garage. Whenever he called her, he didn't expect Pearl to do anything, he just needed someone to hear him out. Six months earlier, when he was changing the flat tire of an eighteen wheeler, he got clumsy and dropped the tire's rim on the left foot of his shop foreman. In that short walk to the telephone, Pearl Debonair also thought maybe, just maybe something happened to her second born son, Will. Even though Will was blessed to survive a troubling birth, he had to take a special medication to deal with seizures that would grab control of his body and mind without any warning. The doctors could not explain Will's condition. Other than the occasional seizure, the boy was fine and the doctors expected the boy would live a normal teenage and adult life. Before she got to the telephone, she had one last thought of panic. What if something happened to Grandma Debonair? That thought left her mind as fast it came. She remembered that Grandma Debonair was a tough lady. Injury and death would know better than to mess with Grandma Debonair. By this time, Mrs. Debonair was tired of her mind playing games and she finally answered the telephone with an urgent, "Hello." Fancy must have felt something was wrong too. As Mrs. Pearl waited for someone to respond on the other end of the telephone, Fancy awoke with a loud cry, "Mama." Mrs. Pearl's mind went in reverse, thinking what in the world is Fancy doing awake; that little girl is supposed to be asleep. Whoever was on the telephone still did not say anything. So, Mrs. Debonair said "Hello" again and followed that with, "Who is it?" A slow, proper and educated voice finally greeted Mrs. Debonair over the telephone. It was the voice of a person who was probably educated at Howard University or Tuskegee. Mrs. Debonair waited to find out who was on the telephone and the reason for their call. While she waited, Fancy screamed even louder, "Mama." Mrs. Pearl didn't want to ignore the cries of her baby. Her mind was on two different important activities. The proper and educated voice introduced herself as Mrs. White. She's the black nurse at the town's elementary school. Ms. Fancy screamed again. Mrs. Pearl asked Mrs. White to hold on. Without waiting for Mrs. White to respond to her request, Mrs. Debonair lowered the telephone receiver to her chest and shouted to Fancy, "Mama will be right with you baby." She then turned her attention back to the telephone, "Hello Mrs. White, what is wrong, are my boys OK?" Mrs. White said, "Well." Mrs. Debonair asked the question again, "Listen lady, are my boys OK?" Because of Will's medical history, she asked about him upfront. "Is my son Will OK?" Mrs. White responded that Will was alright. Mrs. White then continued to say that Stare had to be rushed to the Mountain South Memorial Hospital, which was located on what is now called Martin Luther King Boulevard. Nowadays, almost every county in America has a road, avenue or boulevard named in honor of Martin Luther King. Pearl screamed at Mrs. White, "What happened to my baby? Mrs. White did not take Mrs. Debonair's screaming personally. She was a mother herself and she understood the woman's panic. Mrs. White replied, "I prefer not to say, but the hospital will do everything that it can to help your son." "Right now, I suggest that you and your family head to the hospital. I am so sorry, mam." Mrs. Pearl banged the telephone against the wall to hang it up. With that bang, now the telephone base was leaning one side like the handle on the refrigerator door. Mrs. Pearl promptly dialed her husband at the garage to tell him what little that she knew. She spoke to her husband in parables, broken English and the gibberish of a scared mama. Otis Jr. got the message that something was wrong with one of his boys and that was sufficient to make him leave the garage. His children were his heart. Even though she didn't have to do so, Mrs. Debonair asked her husband to drop whatever he was doing and pick her up at the house. However, she wasn't planning on waiting for her husband to arrive at the house. She nervously placed the telephone in its leaning base. If Ms. Fancy was still calling for her, Mrs. Pearl wasn't able to hear her baby girl. Overrun with concern, Mrs. Pearl headed for Ms. Fancy. She lifted Fancy from the quilts. In one smooth motion, Mrs. Pearl wiped the sleep from Fancy's face with her left hand, put a pair of shoes on her baby and used her right hand to rub the child's hair into a presentable style. Usually, she not allow herself or any of her children to leave the house without looking their best, but this was an exception. She and Fancy headed for the front door. When got on the front porch, she realized that she didn't have her pocketbook. At this point, she was not going back in the house for a pocket book. She did not have any time to lose. Getting to the hospital to check on one of her babies was far more important than a pocketbook with nothing in it.

CHAPTER 5

Otis Jr. and his wife sat on the front porch of their home. As usual, they sat side by side engaged in a lively conversation about their children, finances and business at the garage. It was convenient for the couple to sit side by side as opposed to across from one another. This seating arrangement allowed them to feel closer to one another and they both had a view of Jeremiah and Ms. Fancy as they played in the front yard. Every once in awhile during their discussions, Otis Jr. would lower his voice and whisper something sweet to his wife. His words would cause her to giggle like an over thirty cheerleader. Mrs. Pearl pretended to push her husband away as she fought to contain her giggles. Mrs. Pearl gave birth to five children for him and yet Otis Jr. still took the time to show his wife some innocent affection. Of course, he had to do this when the children were preoccupied. Jeremiah and Fancy played in the twelve by twelve. The yard was of no special grass type. Otis Jr. loved to say, his yard was made up of whatever the good Lord allowed to grow in that space. But, the yard was free of trash and well kept. He managed to keep it cut low enough for the children to bounce around in it. Like the other projects around the family home, Otis Jr. planned to spruce up the yard whenever the family garage made a profit. Right now, he was barely doing enough business to pay his employees and his bills. But, the garage was his dream and Mrs. Pearl was behind him all the way. Mrs. Pearl appreciated the way Otis Jr. referred to the Buick and other stuff as, "The Family's." Meaning, whatever little the family owned, he believed it was shared by all and joint ownership was the rule. He and his wife did not disagree on too many issues of importance. But, on this day, Mrs. Debonair indicated to her husband that maybe he was being a little too hard and demanding on the children. He had recently started taking Fancy to the garage on Saturday's. His wife believed the garage was no place for a young girl. Mrs. Pearl did not mind that the four boys had always spent some time in the garage. Even before they were able to spit out their pacifiers, their father had them in the garage. The boys could not help much, but their father believed that it was never too early to instill a strong work ethic in the boys. His method was paying off. The two oldest boys, Blackmon and Will knew more about running a business and repairing cars than most of the men who relied on their father to keep their cars on the road. You can almost guess that Jeremiah was a different story. He'd be in the garage; however, he'd spend his time talking with the customers about everything and then some. His father complained that Jeremiah did not meet anyone he didn't like or could not talk to. But, Otis Jr. realized that Jeremiah's friendly attitude social skills could be useful as well. As Blackmon and Will acted as deputy automobile surgeons by handing their father different tools when he asked, Jeremiah kept the customers engaged and entertained. His entertainment sometimes caused the customers to forget how long they'd been waiting for their cars to be healed. Mrs. Pearl questioned her husband again, "Why does Fancy have to be in the garage?" Mrs. Pearl wasn't upset. She was only teasing her husband.

She had trust in his methods of dealing with their children. In fact, she knew exactly the response her husband would give. This line of questioning was for a reason that only she knew. So, Otis Jr. gave his wife the sermon that she was after. He asked if he ought to go in the house and pull the lecture seat on the porch. They both laughed. He started, "First off, I don't have much to give our children, so I intend to give them an opportunity to learn a skill that I had to learn the hard way. If nothing else, our children will know the power of an honest days work. They will learn to appreciate things. They will not be beggars. Lastly, "let me remind you that this is part of our plan to raise them the right way so we don't have the misfortune of trying to raise them when they are grown." He interrupted his sermon long enough to tell Jeremiah that he was too close to the Buick. Then he continued, "Honey, when all of these children are sixteen, they are getting out of our house. We are preparing them for that day. Imagine how much you and I can get into with all of the children out of the house and on their own. Fancy will be the last to leave the house. When she leaves, we will paint the house a different color; that way none of them will find us." Mrs. Pearl looked at him out of the corner of her right eye. He went on, "That way, we can have love like the days when we were courting one another." Mrs. Debonair laughed lightly and said, "That sounds good, but you do know the children won't finish school until they are least seventeen. They will be living with us for two years beyond what you expect." He checked on Jeremiah and Ms. Fancy again. This time, they were not too close to the Buick, so he didn't have to say anything to them. He asked his wife, "When did the school board change the graduation age to eighteen?" He was playing with his wife and she knew it. "What about Fancy?" Why do you insist on taking her to the garage?" He thought for a moment and said, "Well, well. "I don't know yet, but I bet you the experience proves to be good for the girl.

Besides, I am trying to balance some of the little woman stuff that you and my mama are putting on Fancy." His wife was surprised that Otis Jr. knew about the activities of Grandma Debonair and Fancy. As the couple thought about calling Jeremiah and Fancy to go inside and prepare for bed, three grown ups and five or so children approached the family's porch. The man who appeared to be the head of the group gave the greeting of the day and proceeded to tell the Debonair's the reason of their visit. His group was preparing for a small civil protest march and they were seeking more adults and children to sign up and participate. Otis Jr. and Pearl listened to the man talk. They did not commit to participating in the protest event, but they told the man that they would consider it.

Chapter 6

Hand in hand and heart to heart, Grandma Debonair and Mr. Henry walked casually to the hospital entrance. Otis Jr. was taking a liking to Mr. Henry; the two men weren't fishing buddies, but they were able to be in the same room together without Otis Jr. feeling uncomfortable. Otis Jr. was still trying to learn more about Mr. Henry. His mama gave Otis Jr. a little information about Mr. Henry, but the information leaks were not fast enough for Otis Jr. Still, Otis Jr. felt surely that his wife knew more about Mr. Henry than he did and his wife still wasn't sharing a whole lot. One thing was for certain, Otis Jr. noticed that whenever his mother was with Mr. Henry, she had the glow of a light bug. Those are the flying bugs that typically emerge in the late summer evenings and their tails light up. Otis Jr. wasn't prepared to do anything that would disrupt his mother's happiness. As they made their way through the hospital entrance, the couple squeezed each other's hand in a playful fashion. It was their day to visit Stare and they were certain that he'd be happy to see them. Stare was in the hospital ever since his frightening fall on the school's playground. His teacher claimed that she doesn't know what or how the fall happened. She said that she turned her back for a quick moment and when she turned again, Stare was on the ground in pain. It all happened so fast, she said. Stare was doing much better no. Initially, the hospital staff was concerned that the boy might be paralyzed. For about week, he could not move either of his legs. The boy must have been born with the same fighting spirit as his paternal grandfather and his brother Will. The medical specialist gave up hope; the boy and his family would not accept the diagnosis. Watching Stare recover was not an easy ordeal for the family. On most days, Mrs. Pearl and Fancy spent their afternoons at the hospital. The hospital became Fancy's afternoon nap place. The hospital was also Fancy's school house and her stage. Fancy, with her cute little self was able to charm every nurse, doctor, janitor, Chaplain and intern in the hospital. The Chaplain included Fancy in every prayer that he offered to the Lord on Stare's behalf. By the way the staff carried on over Fancy, you would think that she was the one who was a patient. Fancy had her fans right where she wanted them. The nurses especially liked to fawn over Fancy's colorful cotton dresses with her matching shoes and socks. Her socks were always rolled down so the flowered edges stood out. The bows in Ms. Fancy's hair were about as many as her Grandma could afford. Grandma would never admit, but she was responsible for Fancy. She didn't give birth to the little girl. But, Grandma Debonair took over for Fancy's appearance right after the child was born. There wasn't much that the family could do for Stare except be there for encouragement and to keep the hospital folks in line. The family was well aware that they had to stay on the hospital staff, otherwise the staff would get lazy and not perform the routine things like change the bed sheets. The family made sure someone was at the hospital every single day. On this particular day, Mr. Henry looked forward to engaging Stare in a game of chess. Mr. Henry wasn't a talkative man, but he was a creative thinker who was also quite successful in business. Not too many folks in town knew about his business success. He was out of business now. He sold everything and moved from New York to Mississippi. Mr. Henry wanted to get away from the big city life. He taught Stare how to play chess in four days. He told Grandma Debonair that Stare was a fast learner and that the boy processed ideas very fast. Mr. Henry was impressed with Stare's attitude and disposition. On more than one occasion, he told the Debonair family that Stare's resilient attitude would cause him to walk again. He was not speaking as a doctor, but speaking as an experienced and wise man. The family made sure that the hospital staff took care of Stare's basic needs as they took care of his emotional needs. Stare never beat Mr. Henry at a single game of chess. Mr. Henry, as competitive as he is, wasn't about to allow the boy to win just because he was young man. He figured that every game of chess with Stare would teach the boy something about life. During the chess games between Mr. Henry and her grandson, Grandma Debonair either spent her time watching the two of them as they matched wits; or she would pace the hospital corridors visiting some of her sick Church sick members. The Church Elders often referred to these folks as the "Sick and shut in." When Grandma Debonair visited any of her ailing Church members, they would always start a conversation with two questions which they delivered like an out of control gas fire. Grandma Debonair didn't mind visiting the sick, but she wished they would shut their mouths when it came to her affairs. Anyway, they'd ask, "Sister Hattimae, why don't we see you at Church as often as we used to and who is this strange man who's been calling on you?" Rather than being thankful that Grandma Debonair took time to visit them like the Good Book says, her sick Church members were trying to find out why she wasn't in Church eight nights a week. Grandma Debonair never answered their questions and she never allowed them to make her feel guilty. She visited with them despite the fact they hey did not seem to appreciate her kindness. No one else from the Church, not even the Pastor or their families even bothered to visit them. Stare never had to go to physical therapy without a family member with him. He didn't moan about the therapy. About the only thing that got on his nerves was when the muscular young man came into his room to interrupt his chess games with Mr. Henry to carry him off to therapy. It almost destroyed the family garage business, but Otis Jr. took off as many days as he could to help care for his son. The bills were piling up, but Otis Jr. and his wife agreed without a second thought that caring for Stare was their priority, no matter the costs. Of course, the family had to consider the escalating hospital costs for Stare's care. Otis Jr. and Ms. Pearl sat around the kitchen table on several mornings staring at the bills and searching for ways to pay for their son's care. All they could do was open the bills each day and shake their heads. Otis Jr. believed the hospital was charging his family for everything except tap water. No matter what it took, they were not going to allow their son to suffer and risk never being able to walk again.

Question of greatness

What is greatness?

How is it measured? How is it determined?

What are the standards for greatness?

How will you know when the definition of greatness?

What is greatness?

What is the root of greatness?

Is greatness a result of suffering, talent,

repetition, luck or diligence?

CHAPTER 7

The Debonair boys, Blackmon, Will and Jeremiah rushed through the front of the family home like three young men who'd had a hard week of work. It was Friday night and they were more than ready to put the school books out of sight and definitely out of mind. Though the weekend was upon them, they were well aware of the family rules, study before play. Yep, even on a Friday evening. So, Will and Jeremiah greeted their mother with a, "Hello mama." She greeted them and pointed for them to head to their bedroom to study. She knew the boys would be wrestling and doing all sorts of things in between their studies. Fancy greeted her brothers as if she were their second mother; instructing them not to get in the way as she and her mother prepared dinner. Stare had recently been released from the hospital. His brothers were surprised to see him at home. They were elated that he was home, but concerned that he still wasn't yet able to do the things with them the way they had before his accident. Stare was making rapid progress though and would resume his normal activities in a few weeks. His physical therapist visited the family home twice a month. Stare reported to his brothers that they better hope to never get sick and have to stay in the hospital. He told them, "The hospital food is tastes bad and they serve applesauce with every meal." The oldest brother, Blackmon was visibly upset about something. Because he was responsible with his studies, he was afforded a little more leeway than his younger brothers. Rather than head to bedroom/study hall, he sat back on the sofa anticipating the arrival of his father. His mother was familiar with the look on Blackmon's face and she knew that he and his father had a routine. If Blackmon had something to discuss with his father, he simply waited for his father to get home so they could talk it out. There were some things that Blackmon shared with his mother. For the most part, Mrs. Pearl accepted that Blackmon was growing older and some issues were best left to his father. Not that she could not handle those issues, it was a family thing. Blackmon sat back on the sofa with his arms crossed with a 'do not mess with me' look on his face. Wouldn't you know it, Fancy found a way to mess with Blackmon despite his unapproachable disposition. She walked right over to her brother, sat down beside him and started chatting away about what she and her mother had been doing all day. "Mama and I did this, Mama and I did that." That went on for five minutes or so before she felt compelled to go bug her mother in the kitchen. She was successful at getting Blackmon to loosen up with a smile. Otis Jr. pulled up in the yard and headed indoors. He had a lot on his mind these days; most of it involving Stare's health, unpaid medical bills and his struggling business. He was still thinking about the Civil Rights activists that visited the home a few weeks earlier. The Civil Rights activists were seeking young and old volunteers to take part in a Protest March. Otis Jr. understood the importance of the purpose, he wanted to help and he wanted to do his part. He did not mind sacrificing. The only problem for he and Mrs. Pearl was whether or not they would allow their children to get involved. There was also the threat to his business that he was worried about. A majority of his white customers threatened that if he took any part in the Protest March, then they would immediately stop giving him their business. He would probably have to close the doors if a majority of his customer chose not to support him. No matter the pressure, he did not allow his wife and children to be affected by any of it. As he walked in the door, he saw Blackmon awaiting his arrival. He imagined what type of issue Blackmon might be experiencing. Otis Jr. put aside his own concerns knowing that he'd have to give Blackmon his undivided attention. Blackmon looked up at his father and greeted him. Otis Jr. greeted Blackmon, Stare, Fancy and his wife all at once. He asked Fancy to come over and get his lunch pale, which Ms. Fancy was glad to do. In a surprise move to Blackmon, his father still wearing his greasy, oil stained clothes asked the boy to join him for a quick walk around the block. First of all, Otis Jr. does not have the snazzy dressing standards of his mother and daughter. However, he rarely goes anywhere between the garage and home in his work clothes. Secondly, he normally drops his tired body in his lecture seat whenever he mentors Blackmon or one of the other boys. Upon hearing her husband ask Blackmon to join him for a walk, Mrs. Debonair kept one eye on Fancy as she lifted the top of a pot to stir the rice and then asked her husband, "Honey are you sure you want to walk around the block in your work clothes?" That was her indirect way of trying to get him to follow his normal routine and stay inside as he spoke with Blackmon. He responded to her question with, "Yeah, I am sure." This must have confused Blackmon because he is so accustomed to hearing his father's advice from a sitting position. Otis Jr. was more concerned about what was on his son's mind than he was concerned about his personal appearance. As the two prepared to leave, Ms. Fancy shouted for them to hurry back because dinner was almost ready. Her mother smiled while thinking Ms. Fancy doesn't know if dinner is five minutes or one hour from being ready. Blackmon and his father headed out and made a sharp right onto the sidewalk. As they headed up the sidewalk, the family's next door neighbors sat on their porch. Otis Jr. greeted his neighbors, but he wasn't in the mood for any extra conversation other than the one he was about to have with his son. Blackmon opened up to his father right away. Blackmon told his father about the upcoming school play. His father said, "Yeah, I know about that" Then Otis Jr. shot is son a couple of questions. "What is the problem?" "Is everything going alright with rehearsal?" The boy was agitated as he continued by telling his father that he would not have the lead role in the play. Blackmon went on, "My teacher, Mr. Russell told me six or seven times and for three weeks that I would have the lead role in the play. "Daddy, Mr. Russell told me a big story. Why did my teacher do that to me? You, mama and Grandma are always telling me to tell the truth and that I should always do the right thing." Otis Jr. asked his son, "Do you have a role in the play?" Blackmon responded that he did have a role, but that role was not the leading role that he was promised by Mr. Russell. The boy was hurt and his father could see his hurt. Otis Jr. placed his arm on his son's shoulders and they walked a few minutes in silence. Otis Jr. started with Blackmon, "Son, it's not the role you play that would make your mama and I proud of you. It is the manner in which you obtain and play that role. "Blackmon, you don't have to have the leading role; your mother and I will be there to support you and be as proud as any parents in the gymnasium." Blackmon responded, "I understand that daddy. But, what about Mr. Russell telling me that big story?" Otis Jr., "Blackmon, I understand your disappointment with Mr. Russell. I can't speak to what made him change his mind and give the role to someone else. I've always told you and your brothers to play the right way. This is a good time for me to tell you the other part of that. And that is, regardless, you must continue to do everything the right way. You can not take it personal or be disappointed when other folks decide not to play the right way, or if they decide to take short cuts by telling stories. You are not responsible for the actions of others, you are responsible for yourself. Sadly Blackmon, this is not the last time that someone will tell you a story. Don't let someone else's story cause you to doubt yourself." Blackmon was cooling off slowly, but he was completely over the situation. He thanked his father and stated that he felt a little better. Otis Jr. was glad to hear his son say that because he was hungry and ready to get out of his musky work clothes.

CHAPTER 8

Based on the unusual number of people moving around inside the Debonair home at 5:45 in the morning, you would think that folks were just getting in from a night of New Year's celebration. It was a new year alright, the first day of a new school year. The Debonair boys were still in their room fussing over whose turn it was to use the hair comb or someone had on their pair of socks. Their mother allowed them to pick their own school clothes. Her only requirement was that their shoes were halfway dusted off. Their pants and shirts didn't have to be color coordinated, but they had to be clean and free of stains. She had to keep her eye on Jeremiah. He pushed her patience as he typically came out of the bedroom wearing pants that showed obvious signs that had recently played in them. Mrs. Pearl would promptly march his butt back in the room to change pants. If he could not find a pair of his own pants, he didn't have any problem with slipping on a pair of Blackmon's pants, which were too big. As he grew bigger and if Blackmon's clothes were still in good shape, Jeremiah would eventually inherit those clothes, but Jeremiah could not wait that long. Jeremiah didn't care if the waist band of his brother's pants hung from his body with enough space to conceal his books. He'd roll up the pant legs in unprofessional cuffs. Mrs. Debonair could only laugh at her youngest son. As far as Jeremiah was concerned, clothes were for playing, other than that, he could do without them. Grandma Debonair insisted on being present so she could ensure that her baby, Ms. Fancy was dressed appropriately for the first day of school. Grandma Debonair had even managed to drag Mr. Henry along with her. He wasn't one for early mornings, but he'd do most anything for Grandma Debonair. The early morning gave him a chance to see his favorite chess pupil, Stare. Mr. Henry had given Stare a cheap chess set. Stare did not know the difference between a cheap and an expensive chess set. He had that cheap chess set with him all the time. No one in the family knew how to play chess. So, if he couldn't play with Mr. Henry, all he could do was practice by himself. Mr. Henry was impressed that Stare had improved so much. For some reason, Ms. Eula was also stalking around the Debonair home. She didn't have any specific purpose or business for being present, except maybe she was searching for some gossip that she could report. That woman could smell free coffee from a different zip code. She was at the Debonair's family kitchen table as she drank coffee like a chocoholic. Ms. Eula was spying on Mrs. Pearl, secretly hoping the woman was pregnant. Otis Jr. and his wife had made a vow that Fancy was the last child for them. Truth be told, Mrs. Pearl made the decision well before her husband did. I mean after the birth of Ms. Fancy, who would want to have any more children? Ms. Belinda, Otis Jr.'s baby sister was also present for duty. She decided to play hooky from her factory job to see the children off to school. She had a ruthless habit of calling in 'ill' to her job. Considering how often she called in ill, it's a wonder that Ms. Belinda still had a job. Let her tell it, she's had every real illness known to mankind; she's even made up a few. Ms.

Belinda and Grandma Debonair were in the bathroom primping and pulling away at Fancy. Every now and then, Ms. Belinda would blast from the bathroom, pull the door closed as if she were protecting a top secret weapon. She went directly to Fancy's dresser drawer in search of a different pair of socks, hair bows or some other apparel. Grandma Debonair was teaching Fancy the fine art of looking pretty on the cheap by not throwing things away until they were too discolored and worn to be recycled. The boys entered the living room, their mother and father had them stand up for inspection. Blackmon really didn't need an inspection. Stare and Will passed the inspection. All three looked well groomed. Poor Jeremiah, he passed inspection his selection of clothes and shoes earned him passing marks. However, the young man had failed to comb his hair. As Jeremiah marched to grease and comb his hair, Mr. Henry, Otis Jr., Mrs. Pearl and Ms. Eula all dropped their heads and covered their mouths to stifle their laughter. Finally, Fancy and her entourage, her two woman posse of Grandma Debonair and her Aunt Belinda entered the living room like a Pop Diva with an attitude on steroids. Fancy stood in the center of the floor for her admirers; Grandma Debonair and Auntie Belinda stood proudly next to her. Otis Jr. dared not say anything. Mrs. Pearl gave Fancy a much different inspection than she would give Jeremiah. Before Fancy was standing in the living room a full ten seconds, her mother moved to embrace the child, "My baby is so pretty." With that, Fancy's inspection was over and the results were certified. Ms. Eula, still in the kitchen guarding the coffeepot, got up from the table for another refill. She said, "I told you all that there is something special about that baby." No one paid her any attention. She said the same thing about every baby that she helped bring into the world, especially if the parents paid her for helping. Mr. Henry smiled at the thought that all of the children were ready for school. Otis Jr. told the children, "Alright, everybody get in the car. It's time to go. Make sure you clean your shoes before you get in the car." Fancy walked over to her daddy, looked up at him and said, "Everything will be alright daddy." Ms. Eula heard what Fancy said and lowered the coffee cup from her thirsty lips in astonishment. Ms. Eula had not been to Church in years, nor had she picked up a Bible in a long time. So, she was known to get her Bible quotes a little mixed up. In reference to Fancy's encouraging words to her father, Ms. Eula announced to the group, "That's just like the Bible says in Mark, Luke or I believe in the book of John." She continued, "It says a child shall rescue them." Grandma Debonair wasn't a Bible scholar herself, but she knew enough about the Bible to know that Ms. Eula was in left field. Grandma Debonair looked at everyone in the room. She took an extra hard look at Ms. Eula and said, "Maybe a better verse and chapter to explain Fancy's encouraging words would be Matthew 11:25." Ms. Eula was in no position to argue or disagree with Grandma Debonair, so she simply said, "Hattimae, you might be right." And, she went back to drinking coffee. She drank the warm coffee as fast as her mouth could stand it. She wanted to enjoy every drop before the family left the house. Otis Jr. wasn't quite sure why Fancy would make such a surprising proclamation, even though it was something that he needed to hear. He bent over his baby girl and thanked her. He then turned to his boys and thanked them. He could only smile as he glanced at Jeremiah who had combed his hair, but his mini Afro was now shiny with an abundance of grease. Otis Jr. looked at his wife and winked at her. The two of them had a date. After dropping the children off at school, Otis Jr. was going to return to the house where he and his wife would dance to the sounds of Smokey Robinson's tune, "I second that emotion." They both had some emotions that needed to be released.

My children got soul

My children got soul

See them move, watch them dance

hear their music, listen to them

as they recite famous Poetic verses and crate

their own

My children got soul

Watch them learn, watch as they

Build something from nothing

Energetic, intelligent and Bold

My children got soul

CHAPTER 9

"Ice cream, ice cream, daddy's taking us to get some ice cream." Fancy and all four of her brothers were in the car with their father as they headed for the west side of town for ice cream. Usually, Fancy would stretch herself to reach for the radio dial as she would turn the knob in search of Soul music. On this day, she and her brothers were preoccupied making their own music as they sang, "Ice cream, ice cream, daddy's taking us to get some ice cream." The trip was a family ritual. Their mother, Mrs. Pearl never made the trips. She stayed at home and took full advantage of the time that her children were away. She loved her children dearly, but she loved them even more whenever she could get a well deserved break all to herself. Before he and the children left the house, Otis Jr. would ask his wife, "Honey, what do you do when the children and I are gone?" Her standard response to his inquiry was the same, "Honey, I do stuff." Then he'd ask, In his desire for specifics, he'd ask his wife, "What type of stuff do you do?" Mrs.Pearl would stand her ground by repeating her previous answer, "Honey, I do the stuff that I have to do." So, Otis Jr. jokingly accused his wife of entertaining her boyfriend in his absence. To which, Mrs. Debonair did not deny or reject the accusations. She must have learned this from Grandma Debonair. But, she and her husband both knew that hew was the only man that she enjoyed dancing with him. Fancy sat in the front of the car, between her father and Jeremiah. Her short legs dangled from the seat, not yet long enough to reach the car floor. She and Jeremiah used their upper bodies to push and shove one another. Fancy was fifteen or so pounds lighter than Jeremiah, but she held her own in the shoulder pushing contest. Now and again, Ms. Fancy would stealthily push her right leg in a modified kick of Jeremiah. Jeremiah didn't mind Fancy's girlish violence, he enjoyed his baby sister. As Otis Jr. held the Buick on the narrow, two lane road, he glanced over at Ms. Fancy and Jeremiah with a look that asked them to quit their activities. He'd say to Ms. Fancy, "Girl, your brother is bigger than you, what do you think you are going to do with him?" Blackmon, Will and Stare sat in the back seat of the car wondering which lecture their father had prepared for them today. As they waited for their father to introduce today's lecture, the children continued to sing their ice cream song. Blackmon and Stare were on to the trickery of their father. They knew full well that the trips to the ice cream house were more than about the special, sweet taste of Butter Pecan, Berry Strawberry and Creamy Vanilla. The boys knew their father would eventually unleash one of his fire and brimstone lectures about life. Sure enough, as Otis Jr. pulled the Buick up to the ice cream house, he said to the children that today's lesson was about fairness. His announcement was perfect timing. The children could already taste the ice cream and they were in a cooperative mood. Some folks might call this manipulation, but Otis Jr. called it quality family time. Jeremiah, Blackmon and Will opened the car doors. Their father asked them all to be careful. Jeremiah got out of the car, he held the door open for his sister. Ms. Fancy slid her little self over to the car door and climbed out of the automobile like a trained young lady. Her legs were close together, her head moved up and down slowly to make sure her feet touched the ground. She thanked her brother for holding open the door, to which he did not respond. Jeremiah used both of his hands and the strength of his legs to push the car door closed. Then, he dashed away to make sure he was the first one in line. Otis Jr. could just see the miniature handprints that Jeremiah left all over the car door. After ordering their ice cream, the family sat outside waiving at folks that they did not know and some who were customers at Mr. Debonair's garage. You couldn't tell Fancy that some folks were strangers; she acted as if she recognized every passerby and they better know her too. The children licked away at their ice cream cones. Fancy and Jeremiah had to wipe their mouths quite often. They weren't able to lick the ice cream as fast as the warm weather did damage to it. Their father continued with his lecture about fairness. As if to get the lecture off on the right foot, Fancy asked her father, "What does fair mean daddy?" Otis Jr., "Baby, fair would be like what we are doing right now. All of us came to the ice cream house and we all have ice cream." He continued, the opposite of fair would be that we all came to the ice cream store and only you got to eat ice cream and not your brothers." Jeremiah cut his eyes at Fancy. Fancy responded that it would be alright with her if she were the only one that got to eat ice cream. That's when the other boys all moaned, No, it wouldn't be alright" Otis Jr. was tickled by their verbal exchange. He had to get his lecture back on track. He gathered himself and continued. He looked directly at his three older boys; "Listen, sometimes in this life, you will get what you think you deserve. On the flip side, very often you will get less than you think deserve and sometimes you won't get anything at all." He watched their faces and allowed his words to circulate in their minds. He was pretty sure that Blackmon would be able to put it together. Blackmon asked, "Daddy, is that like when I did not get the lead role in the school play?" Otis Jr. had to think about his son's question momentarily. He responded to Blackman, "Yes son, it is." Otis Jr. finished the day's lecture with, "Sometimes, life and people will treat you fairly. At other times, you will feel as though you are being treated unfairly. No matter how you are treated, don't allow any situation to make you lose your dignity and self-confidence. Otis Jr. realized that he would have to explain the word dignity at a later date. Lastly, he said to the children, "Don't allow any of life's challenges to fill your hear with lasting bitterness. Ms. Fancy wasn't paying much attention to her father. Sensing the end of her father's lecture, she said, "My daddy is so smart." She had finished her ice cream and was laying the ground work to ask for more. She burst out singing a new version of their ice cream song. "Ice cream, ice cream, Daddy is going to buy me some ice cream."

CHAPTER 10

Early one morning before the Angels of Heaven had a chance to perform their personal hygiene, Mrs. Pearl and Otis Jr. sat at the family kitchen table discussing how the children were doing in school. They also discussed what kind of financial shape the garage was in, their bills, especially the bill for Stare's medical treatment and whether or not they'd allow the children to take part in the upcoming Protest March. These early morning meetings for the pair were a common occurrence just like the evening family dinners. The family dinner was not about food, but dinner was an opportunity for the parents to get the latest on their children. Mrs. Pearl did not take offense that the children thought Grandma Debonair was a much better cook than she was. Aside from satisfying their nutritional needs, Mrs. Pearl prepared dinner as a way to get the inside scoop on her children directly from her children. And, as the children ate, they tended to tell on one another. Amongst themselves, they would ask each other, "Why did you tell mama or daddy that I did…?' As far as his children's education, Otis Jr. was not overly concerned with the three older boys, Blackmon, Stare and Will.

He and his wife didn't have to get on Blackmon a whole lot. But, Stare and Will needed to be put in check every now and again. On the whole, the boys were putting in the effort to be good students. On the other hand, Jeremiah cared about school as much as he cared about greasing and combing his hair. You know the story on him. It was to his advantage that his parents gave him constant reassurance through the rod. Mrs. Pearl and Otis Jr. continued their morning discussion over warm black coffee. Mrs. Debonair had one very important topic and two important letters that she desperately wanted to share with her husband. Otis Jr. had one important issue that he wanted to get off of his chest. Mrs. Pearl went first, "Otis, promise me that you won't get upset when I show you this letter and give me a chance to explain the circumstances. Your mother and I have taken care of it. In fact, your mother went to the school before I even had a chance to do so." Otis Jr. mumbled, "I promise." Mrs. Debonair had heard him say that before. What she was about to tell him involved Fancy and a teacher who discouraged the child from dreaming of becoming an engineer. Mrs. Pearl knew from previous experience that her husband would not tolerate a soul that attempted to stifle or discourage any of his children. So, his promise to be cool was a waste of time. Mrs. Debonair removed the folded letter from the pocket of her sagging bath robe. The bathrobe that Otis Jr. and the children purchased for her on Mother's day three years earlier. She didn't like the bath robe, but she wore it because her children and husband bought it and they were overjoyed to deliver it to her. She believed that some gifts were more special than others. She handed her husband the letter. He took off his glasses so he'd be able to read the letter. He needed his glasses to drive, but for some odd reason, he couldn't read with them. Mrs. Pearl asked her husband when he was going to take time to get an eye exam. Maybe it was time for him to look into getting a pair of bifocals. He responded, "I can read fine without bifocals." He never did answer his wife's question about getting an eye exam. He unfolded the letter and took in the words. As best she could, Mrs. Pearl prepared herself for his certain strong reaction. Otis Jr. read the letter in silence as his wife watched his eyes closely. As he neared the end of the letter, she placed a hand on his shoulder and said, "Baby, its nothing to worry about." His anger in the early stages, he responded to his wife, "I'll be the judge to determine whether this is something to get excited about or not. Those were the words of a man who was about explode. After Otis Jr. finished reading the letter, he stood up quickly, nearly lifting the table with his quadriceps muscles and causing coffee to spill from his cup. His wife was holding her cup in her free hand. Otis Jr. asked his wife, "What in the hell do these people at that school mean by telling my baby that she should not set her goals of becoming an engineer? Don't they realize that is our baby?" He wasn't asking a question, he was just stating a fact. He didn't expect his wife to answer. He voice wasn't loud but it was forceful, "If our baby desires to dream of becoming an engineer, then they damn well better let her dream and not discourage her. Those folks don't have any right to tell Fancy that she should focus her attention on being somebody's house keeper. Now, if Fancy decides to become a domestic that will be her choice. She will not accept something less than her dreams simply because someone from that doggone school tries to steer her in that direction." He was saying all of this, but in the back of his mind he was wondering, "An engineer, where did Fancy get such a big idea? How Fancy got the idea to become an engineer was nowhere near as important as folks trying to steer her in an opposite direction. Otis Jr. figured that his mama, his wife and his younger sister all had something to do with Fancy's engineering dream. As he steamed with anger, Mrs. Pearl stood up with him, hoping that he would not wake the children. "Honey, we took care of it. It won't happen again." He calmed down a bit and said,

"Those school folks don't want me to show up at that school." Mrs. Debonair was glad that conversation was over. She was certain that her next topic would be good news for her husband. The two of them sat back down. Before he let go of the topic, Otis Jr. uttered, "I can't believe this." His wife said, "I can't believe that you lied to me. You said that you would not loose your cool over this letter." He said, "Honey, you know full well that I will always loose my coold when it comes to these children." Then he started the next discussion. "Baby, I don't know what we are going to do about the medical costs for Stare. I realize that the hospital wants all of the outstanding payment, but maybe if I go down and talk with them again, maybe they will allow us to continue making payments until the entire bill is paid in full. Hell, the boy still has a slight limp." Just as her husband finished making this statement, Mrs. Pearl reached into the other pocket of her special bath robe and pulled out another letter. This letter was from the hospital's finance department. Mrs. Pearl smiled as she presented her husband with this letter. She knew exactly what the letter stated. So, she had no need to prepare herself for her husband's manly display of anger. The thought of being in the red for seven thousand dollars to the hospital caused Otis Jr. to lower his head in his cupped hands and stare through the table for a solution that was not available. Sensing the inevitable bad news, he tried to cut through the chase and eventual frustration by asking his wife to tell him what the letter said. She would not tell him. He asked her, "Are you really going to make me read some more bad news?" Mrs. Pearl didn't say a word. She handed him the letter which was folded as neat and wrinkle free as the day the hospital mailed it out. The letter from the school looked as though it had been trampled over and peed on by a neighborhood mutt. Otis Jr. cautiously took possession of the letter and started reading. Dear so and so... He skipped around some words and got to the bottom where it said, Paid in Full, Thank you for your payment. This time he could not stand up, he had no reason to rattle the kitchen table in his anger. His legs, arms, chest and back were to overcome with shock for him to lift himself from the table. He asked his wife a series of rapid fire questions; questions that came out of his mouth so fast that Mrs. Pearl didn't have an opportunity to respond. He started with, "Honey, is this letter for real?" "What do they mean by paid in full?" How'd the bill get paid?" He went on, "Who, why and when?" Mrs. Debonair had some answers, but she could not answer who, why and when. She said to him, "Look, I am not like your son Jeremiah, I do my homework." She only said "your son Jeremiah" to make fun of Jeremiah's unwillingness to do his schoolwork. Otis Jr. laughed and said, "Alright now, leave my boy alone." Mrs. Pearl went on, "I called the hospital to make sure the letter was authentic. I asked several employees in the finance department if they knew who paid that large sum on our family's behalf. The hospital staff said they could not give me that information. Well aware of his mother's fixed income situation, Otis Jr. knew there was no way that he could hold her directly responsible for this good fortune. Just then, Fancy and Will trying to shake off sleep, entered the living room expressing their morning hunger. Otis Jr. looked at his watch realizing he had to race to the garage. Like he learned from Ms.Eula, he took one last sip of what used to be warm coffee. He swallowed the coffee and headed for the door. Finally having some goods and better luck, he abruptly turned around to kiss Mrs. Pearl and two of his children who only had breakfast on their minds. There was no need for the conversation on whether the children would be allowed to take part in the protest march. However, Otis Jr. managed to escape the house without talking to his wife about the topic that really burned inside of him. He had a few more weeks before he had to break down and come up with a way to tell her what he was keeping buried in his heart.

CHAPTER 11

Any other day, another time, Otis Jr. would go straight home after work. On this afternoon though, he decided to take a detour to Slim's Pool Hall. He hadn't visited the pool hall in several years. This short detour in the pool hall would give him opportunity to escape, relax and reason with himself. Back in the day, the day before he became a dedicated family man and business owner; Otis Jr. was a pretty good pool player. Or, as the older guys referred to him, he was a hustler. Otis Jr. started shooting pool when he was twelve years old. The pool hall wasn't a place for him to be, but he managed to find his way in and picked up some good habits as well as some bad. This afternoon, he was involved in a game and had his victim or opponent hoping that he'd miss a shot. Otis Jr. stood over the pool table like a predator animal tracking his next meal. If he could sink the next three balls, the win would put ten dollars in his pocket. That would be enough money to buy himself and his buddies a round of chilled beer. Still leaning over the pool table, his eyes glittered with a strategy. He stood straight up and reached for the chalk to lubricate the end of his stick. The only trouble that Otis Jr. expected was getting the cue-ball from the awkward position where it rested. Now, he had a plan. He bent back over the table and went to work. Ain't it funny how a true hustler like Otis Jr. never loses his gifts? Otis Jr. had his pool stick cocked and ready and his mental strategy all mapped out. He called out to his victim, "Seven ball in the corner pocket." The seven ball was obedient to Otis Jr.'s command, it went down like the temperature on the first day of winter. Otis Jr.'s victim could do nothing but try to look unfazed, try to put on portrait of confidence. The only confidence in the room belonged to Otis Jr. He was confident that his buddy would be buying a round of beer. Otis Jr. moved over behind the eight-ball. He announced, "Eight-ball in the side pocket." The eight ball snaked around the nine-ball in perfect movement, just the kind of luck or skill that Otis Jr. needed to get closer to ending the game. With the disappearance of the eight ball, Otis Jr. could taste the free beer. The only two balls that were left on the table were the nine-ball and of course the cue-ball. Otis Jr. shifted quickly to analyze the situation. He had to get the nine-ball to roll left to right and to the opposite end of the table. He was confident; so confident that he started really talking trash to his buddy. "Man, it is sure nice to be gone for years and walk in off the streets and earn some easy money." As he pointed to the far left corner of the pool table, he said, "The nine-ball is going to fall right there. I can close my eyes and make this one." His victim said, "Man, stop talking all the smack and shoot pool." Otis Jr. pulled the trigger on his pistol of a pool stick. The cue-ball made solid contact with the nine-ball, the nine-ball snaked towards the pocket that Otis Jr. had pointed out. The green liner on the pool table was not in perfect condition, it had bumps and tears from over use. One of the bumps in the pool table cause the nine ball to skip off course just a little. Even with that skip, the nine-ball managed to stay on target as it continued towards a familiar pocket and home. Ot

Jr. and his playing victim watched as the nine-ball moved over the pool table as if it had a radar device directing it to the pocket. Down went the nine-ball, "Game over man, buy us some beers." Otis Jr. won the game, but he believed in sharing free beer with everyone in the pool hall. As the game ended, Otis Jr. noticed Mr. Henry standing nearby. The two men shook hands and moved to a semi-quiet area of the pool hall. There's no such thing as a private space in a pool hall. Their beers were delivered to the table by a young man who looked about the same age as Otis Jr. when he first started hanging out in the pool hall. The boy wasn't old enough to drink, but he was old enough to try and hustle up a few dollars. The conversation between Otis Jr. and Mr. Henry started with small talk about the Debonair children. Mr. Henry mentioned that Stare had become quite a chess player and that he enjoyed teaching the boy. Otis Jr. responded that Stare was indeed a chess player and that Stare was now trying to teach him how to play. Otis Jr. admitted that Stare's efforts to teach him how to play chess was like using a crescent wrench when a job calls for a hammer. The two men laughed. Then Mr. Henry asked about the other children. Otis Jr. said they were all doing alright. He added, "That Fancy is something else." Mr. Henry quickly agreed that Fancy was something else. Neither ne of the men could figure out what Fancy was, but they agreed that ⁚ was something else. Mr. Henry remembered how Ms. Fancy ᵐmed everyone on the hospital staff. Otis Jr. needed to talk some He started with the easy stuff. He would even practice with Mr. on what he desperately needed to share wit his wife. He told Mr. ʰen he first started shooting pool and how long it was since he d the pool hall. Mr. Henry was a quite man, but he was 1 in the streets. He was not surprised by Otis Jr.'s statement ᵉd shooting pool at an age when he should have been s ᵴ studies. Otis Jr. was a little hesitant, but he recognized that he needed to get this issue in the open. He told Mr. Henry that one of the customers from his garage had stopped by early one morning for a classified talk. The customer stopped by before he had a chance to open the garage for business. This is what Otis Jr. wanted to tell his wife a few days earlier, but avoided doing so. He didn't want his wife to worry. Anyway, Otis went on by telling Mr. Henry the rest of story. He said that the customer told him that he should not get involved with this Protest March because something bad could happen. Otis said he asked the man to be frank. "What do you mean something bad could happen?" "First off, the man said, if you decide to take part in this Protest March foolishness, some of your other customers and I may decide not to support your garage any loner. "Further, if you get involved with the Protest March, losing our business may be the least of your worries." Otis Jr. said the man finished that last statement and turned to walk out of his garage. Otis Jr. noticed that the man's first statement was frank. But, his second statement was left wide open. He did not know how to break the code or interpret the man's last statement. He stopped talking to Mr. Henry for a minute and took an extra swig of beer. After he absorbed the idea that his business was threatened and swallowing a mouth full of beer, Otis Jr. lowered the bottle from his lips. He let out a breath of air as if he was in disbelief, but at the same time he was relieved. He did not place his beer bottle on the table because as soon as he swallowed that first swig of beer, he took another swig. Otis Jr. continued, "I don't know what the gentleman meant by "Losing his business will be the least of my worries." Otis Jr. told Mr. Henry, "I can't afford to worry about it either. "Next week, my family and I are going to take part in that Protest March." Mr. Henry took a sip of beer. He didn't need to take a swig. Then he asked Otis Jr. if he thought it was a wise idea to get involved in the Protest March? Otis Jr. responded, "My wife and I have thought about it and discussed this issue up and down. The way we figure it, the world is a changing place and we won't be able to protect our children all of the time. But, we want the children to understand that they have to have principles and that they must stand up for the things that they believe. Lastly, I figure this Protest March is a good opportunity to give the children a real life experience." Mr. Henry listened intently to Otis Jr., He said, "OK, I am not trying to change your mind young brother or question your judgment. From what I hear you saying, it sounds like you are prepared to make whatever sacrifices are required as a result of your convictions." Mr. Henry continued by saying, "You know what young man, I've had as much good luck in my life as I've had bad luck. I don't take my good luck or good fortune for granted. But, but brother I sure could have done without the bad luck." The two men exchanged smiles. Mr. Henry went a little further by saying, "Seriously, even my bad luck has made me a better man." He finished by saying, "Good luck or bad, it is best to take what comes your way and don't ask a lot of unnecessary questions." Otis Jr. nodded in agreement as he thought about the recent good luck that his family had when he learned that a Samaritan paid the balance of Stare's medical bills. He reflected on Mr. Henry's words and the reason Mr. Henry was probably telling him stories about good luck and bad luck. Otis Jr. thought to himself, maybe Mr. Henry was the one who paid those medical bills. Otis Jr. briefly considered asking Mr. Henry if he knew anything about the medical bills being paid. But, his mind got stunned with what Mr. Henry said about taking what comes your way and not asking too many unnecessary questions. Determined to leave his beer bottle completely empty, no visible liquid or suds; Otis Jr. turned up the bottle and drank what little beer was left. Though he had earned a second beer, he did not have time for it. Otis Jr. had a hot date with his wife. Later in the evening he and Mrs. Peal were going to a juke joint for dancing. He could picture his wife and

Fancy as they rumbled through his wife's outfits searching for a perfect dress, a pair of shoes and matching pocketbook. Ms. Fancy took great interest in giving her mother fashion advice. Otis Jr. told Mr. Henry that he had to leave. Mr. Henry knew about Otis Jr.'s hot date because Grandma Debonair had asked him to go with her and sit with the Debonair children. Otis Jr. thanked Mr. Henry for his company and conversation, saying both were just what he needed. He walked out of the pool hall with a lot more determination than when he walked in and his renewed determination wasn't because of the free beer. As he left, Otis Jr. hollered at his buddies that he'd be back to collect on the remaining beers and to take some more of their money. In reality, he was a family man and he had no idea when he'd be able get to the pool hall again.

CHAPTER 12

Apprehension and excitement were in the air. Mrs. Pearl Debonair was excited at the idea of going out with Otis Jr. for an evening of dancing. As she and Fancy put the final touches on her evening wear, Mrs. Debonair kept repeating to herself, "Free entertainment. An evening of dancing with my handsome husband and enjoying the free entertainment provided by the other dancing couples." The free entertainment would come in the form of couples dancing as if they were in the privacy of their own bedrooms. On the dance floor, Mrs. Pearl would whisper to Otis Jr. and nod her head in the direction of a dirty dancing couple. She'd say to Otis Jr. "Look over there, you see that?" Or the entertainment might come from seeing a woman wearing a dress that was way too tight, too colorful or plain ugly. Mrs. Pearl always got a good laugh from the gentlemen that drank themselves silly and fell asleep at their tables while their female companions took to the arms of sober men. Otis Jr. went out of his way to make Mrs. Pearl feel special. He made it his goal to make her feel like she was being courted and he was successful at that. Mrs. Pearl understood that the world was a serious place with serious issues. She also took advantage of every opportunity to enjoy life's inexpensive pleasures. Tonight would be great. But, there was no telling what tomorrow would bring. She was married to Otis Jr. long enough to know that while he agreed to allow the children to participate in the Protest March, he was still concerned about what could happen. He did not have to tell her these things, she knew. Mrs. Pearl had girlfriends who resided in other Southern towns who'd telephone her often to say protestors were not welcomed in their respective communities. Those girlfriends would tell her that the protestors were greeted with the red carpet of physical violence issued out by angry mobs as well as the uncomfortable amenities of a cold and crowded jail cell. Nevertheless, while she did not expect such an unfriendly reception in her own town; she and Otis Jr. would have to prepare the children in case got out of hand. Mrs. Pearl diverted her mind away from the Protest March. After trying on three different outfits, Mrs. Debonair had finally decided on the dress that was the least revealing. She did not want to wear anything to tight or revealing, she figured her womanly stuff was for Otis' viewing only; other gentlemen would just have to use their imagination. Besides, most of her clothes had not been updated since she gave birth to Jeremiah. Her body didn't carry too much baby birthing gain. In fact, Otis Jr. had convinced her that she looked outstanding for a woman who'd given birth to five children. She laughed at the thought that her husband had a way of making her feel as though she was the only girl at the dance. She took to admiring herself in the small mirror of their dresser drawer. Still looking in the mirror, she gazed at the family photo that rested on the night stand. She was proud of her family. Grandma Debonair was already at her son's home; she waited with the boys in the living room. Blackmon had placed Grandma Debonair's purse and other belongings in their usual hiding place. Fancy had on one of her mother's smaller and form fitting dresses. So, with her mother beside and holding her hand, Fancy walked pigeon toed from her parents bedroom. As the two of them reached the front door, the boys laughed at Fancy and told their mama how beautiful she looked. Mrs. Debonair received an unexpected applause from Grandma Debonair. However, that did not keep Grandma Debonair from leaving her seat to make a few minor corrections to Mrs. Debonair's choice of jewelry. As for Fancy, Grandma Debonair asked the child, "Girl, what do you have on? Just what do you think you are wearing?" Fancy gave her best profile and responded to her Grandma that, "I look pretty like mama." Grandma could only say, "Okay then." Mrs. Debonair went ahead and thanked Grandma Debonair again for taking time to care for the children while she and Otis Jr. went out to enjoy themselves. Grandma Debonair recognized that her son and his wife needed to get out of the house as a way to maintain their relationship. Otis Jr. walked in a few minutes later. He only needed a short time to shower and dress. His wife always picked out his dress clothes. He walked in and asked Blackmon to remove himself for his lecture seat. Before he did anything else, Otis Jr. wanted to discuss the Protest March with the children. Noticing that his wife was dressed and looking pretty, he winked at her slyly. He gave her the kind of wink that said, I am so proud that you are my woman. He asked Fancy to sit her little self down. As Fancy squeezed on the sofa between her Grandma and Stare, she asked her daddy what he thought of her outfit. Upon hearing Fancy's question Otis Jr., the rest of the family started laughing hysterically. They may have been laughing, but Ms. Fancy was serious. She expected a response from her daddy. She waited patiently for her daddy to answer. Otis Jr. did his best to contain his own laughter bone and told his daughter that she looked every bit as sweet as her mother. Grandma Debonair was tickled that Otis Jr. managed to avoid hurting Fancy's feelings.

Mrs. Pearl and Grandma Debonair looked at each other, they looked at the ceiling and the floor then they covered her mouths as they attempted to muffle their giggles. Otis Jr. started the discussion by calling each child's name, from the oldest to the youngest. It was almost like he was taking roll call. All of the children responded, "Yes, daddy." Otis Jr. went on, "…something about Protest March, better opportunities and equality. Blackmon surprised his father and mother by saying, "Daddy we know all about that Protest March stuff. A woman came to our school to talk about it." Otis Jr. was confident that his three oldest, Blackmon, Stare and Will had ideas about the purpose behind the Protest March. He did not expect them understand completely, just have an idea. Otis Jr. continued to tell the children that the Protest March was taking place in the morning. He asked them if they wanted to go. Before any of the boys could answer, Fancy said, "Yes, we want to go." Fancy response would lead you to think that she was the elected spokesperson for the boys too. Then all the boys said in unison that they also wanted to go. Otis Jr. told the children that people might be mean to them, spit at them and maybe even try to put them in jail. But, he and their mama would do everything in their power to protect them. He asked them again, "Do you all still want to go?" Ms. Fancy asked, "What time are we leaving home?" Otis Jr. said, "Hold on baby, I want to make sure you all understand what this is about and what could happen." "None of you have to go." Now, he was sounding as if he was trying to scare the children or convince them not to go. Grandma Debonair spied on each child's face, searching for any signs of doubt. The children still said that they wanted to go. It was not as if the children had the final say on whether or not they would attend the Protest March. If Otis Jr. and his wife though it would be dangerous for the children, they would not be allowed to attend. Otis Jr. understood that his children were probably consumed with a smidgen of naivety. However, having done all he could to scare them about the possibilities, he admired their youthful courage. "OK", he said, "We will leave here at seven in the morning." Grandma Debonair said to her son, "I don't want anything to happen to these boys and my future engineer." Fancy lit up because she knew her Grandma was talking about her. "That's right daddy, I am going to be an engineer." Otis Jr. pushed himself up from his lecture seat, stood up and told his mother that nothing would happen to the children. As he headed to the backroom, he reminded his wife how gorgeous she looked and said he was going to get ready for their evening out. Fancy wiggled out of her seat as she said to her father that she was going to help him. There wasn't much Ms. Fancy could do to her father, Mrs. Pearl Debonair had laid her husband's clothes, right down to his socks. Mrs. Pearl was ready to go, she was already picturing herself in Otis Jr.'s arms on the dance floor. She did not know what tomorrow would bring, but she was certainly ready to spend the evening dancing and laughing.

That little girl

That little girl

That little knows exactly where she

wants to go and what she wants to accomplish

That little girl even knows who she wants on her team

Her team

That little girl

That little girl has her life all mapped out, from her prom

& wedding gowns to how she'll spend the evening

celebrating her 25th bride and groom anniversary

That little

That little girl thinks she's prepared to handle

a perfect blend of adversity, disappointment, accomplishment

and joy

That little girl

CHAPTER 13

The Protest March. The day of the Protest March had arrived. The Debonair family had quick breakfast and they were all set to leave the house. Taking her usual seat, Fancy settled in the family car as well as the other family members. The Debonair boys took their places in the back seat. Blackmon and Stare sat near the doors like a couple of well trained soldiers who were pulling their shifts of guard duty. The drive to the March would take them by their automobile repair garage. Following her musical instincts, Fancy reached to turn on the car radio. It was appropriate that a sweet tune by Otis Redding was oozing through the in-dash stereo. Fancy twisted the tune knob until the sounds came through as clear and perfect as she could get it. The third chorus of Brother Redding's song played without static. "I go to a movie, and I go downtown. Somebody keep telling me don't hang around. It's been a long time coming. But I know a change is gonna come." The song was appropriate for the occasion. As the song continued to play, Otis Jr. looked down at Fancy with a proud smile on his face. He was pleased that Ms. Fancy adopted his love and appreciation for music. In the voice and spirit of an old train conductor, Otis Jr. announced to the family, "Is everyone ready?" The children shouted that they were ready. Otis Jr. placed the car in reverse, threw his right arm over the top of the front seat and then backed slowly out of the driveway onto the quiet street. "A change is gonna come." The words rang through his mind over and over. After all that the nation had endured, Otis Jr. had no way of knowing how much additional destruction, personal strife and sacrifice would be required to bring about change. As he drove, he had time to consider this, but he knew that there was no turning back. The car bounced to a halt at an intersection. Mrs. Debonair had a serious but light mood. She thought about the previous evening that she and Otis Jr. spent at the juke joint. She remembered that her husband looked wonderful and he still danced with the grace and strut of a frightened Ostrich. She really enjoyed herself. And, Otis Jr. kept his word by making her feel like they were courting as opposed to a stale husband and wife cohabitation where both are waiting on death. About the only draw back to an evening in the juke joint was the awful smell of cigar and cigarette smoke. In a strange way, Mrs. Pearl enjoyed the sweet smell of a gentleman smoking a pipe. After every dance, Mrs. Debonair would hang her dress and Otis Jr.'s suit on the back porch so the clothes could get some fresh air. There was no way that she could hang those clothes in the closet until they were free of the tobacco scent. As her husband continued guiding the car towards their destination, her mind drifted to the advice that Grandma Debonair had once given her. Well, there really was more than one piece of worthy advice that Grandma Debonair had given her. In fact, Grandma Debonair had taken a liking to her well before the couple decided to marry. But, it was Grandma Debonair who'd coached the young woman on how to corral a young stud like Otis Jr. Mrs. Debonair laughed as she thought about those days. The other tidbit of advice that she received from Grandma Debonair was a little more significant. Grandma Debonair told her that often times personal sacrifice is required but the actual payment is called when one is least prepared to pay it. The payment could be demanded in various forms, our lives, someone that we love, limb or personal property. Grandma Debonair, "Pearl, if you live long enough, you will have make more than one sacrifice; that just comes with living. Mrs. Debonair could only reflect on that advice and hope her payment day would never come. Thus far, she and her family were blessed. One of the boys interrupted her thoughts, "Mama, when are we going to get there?" She responded that they would get there soon enough. As Otis Jr. continued guiding the car, he and his wife could see a dark cloud of smoke up ahead. The couple glanced at each other with faces of worry. The family was still four blocks away from their automobile garage. Otis Jr. hated to think that the cloud of smoke had something to do with the planned Protest March. He quickly put that thought out of his mind and sang "A change is gonna come – even though the song had long stopped playing on the radio. He sang that one phrase over and over. He was so into Otis Redding's verse that he didn't notice the song was no longer playing. Fancy nodded her head up and down as her father sang that one chorus repeatedly. The closer the car got to the area where the family's garage was located, the more Otis Jr. and his wife feared what may lie ahead. The thick smoke rose into the morning air like a thief climbing out of his neighbor's window. The smoke was in a hurry to get somewhere - anywhere besides the site of destruction. At this point, Otis Jr. was no longer concerned about the Protest March. He was forced to stop the car one block away from the scene of the fire. Seemed like everyone that had plans to take part in the Protest March were standing around gazing at the fire as it engulfed concrete, sheet rock, rubber and plaster. By this time, Otis Jr. realized that it was the family's garage that was on fire. He pounded his fist against the steering wheel so hard that it caused his wife to hold her chest in surprise. Ms. Fancy sat straight as she tried to see over the dashboard of the car. The boys scrambled in the back seat, they could not see what was going on. Blackmon asked, "What's wrong daddy? Why are we stopping?" Otis Jr. replied, "Nothing, you all sit here till I get back." He jumped out of the car, pushed the door closed, bent over and told his wife that everything would be alright. Mrs. Pearl forced a look of cool on her face. Her instincts told her that everything would not be alright. Then it dawned on Mrs. Pearl that maybe this was her family's moment of sacrifice. The words, the advice about sacrifice that she had received from Grandma Debonair now had meaning and purpose. It was sorta like they say about the Bible, "It is the living Word of God. You know, the scriptures make sense; but the scriptures seem to come to life whenever a Child of God finds himself or herself in an hour of despair. Otis Jr. pushed the car door closed and started off to make his way through the crowds. Before he could get too far away, Fancy screamed, "Can I go daddy? "I wan to help you." Otis Jr. responded, 'No, baby you can't go. Stay in the car and help your mama and brothers. Daddy will be right back." He started to push his way through the crowd. He asked himself what could have started a fire at the family's business? Did the fire have something to do with a threat made by one of his customers? He did not have any answers to his questions. As he got to the front of the crowd, he ran into his mama, Mr. Henry and Ms. Eula who was standing a few feet away. The three of them were standing helplessly, their spirits cloaked in defeat. Her eyes full of tears and her handkerchief unable to absorb any more tears, Grandma Debonair embraced and consoled her son. Mr. Henry stood next to Grandma Debonair, his arm wrapped around her waist. For Mr. Henry, the fire and smoke was a sad reminder of one that he'd experienced thirty years earlier. With her anxiety running on overload, Mrs. Pearl could not wait in the car any longer. She grabbed her pocketbook and Fancy's in one smooth move. She started to push open the car door while yelling instructions to the boys, "You boys get out of the car. Blackmon, you hold Jeremiah's hand; Stare, you hold Will's hand and you all stay close behind me." She and the children fought their way through the rows of people. As Mrs. Pearl and the children made their way closer to the fire, some of the bystanders attempted to say words of encouragement and support. Mrs. Pearl didn't hear a word that was said to her. Her mind was on getting to the front to see exactly what was going on. Besides, what words are able to encourage a family when their livelihood and there very source of shelter and food is reduced to ashes? After a walk that seemed like several miles, Mrs. Pearl and the children finally reached the spot where Otis Jr. stood with Grandma Debonair, Mr. Henry and Ms. Eula. Everyone's face was wet from either crying or sweating in the summer heat. Mrs. Pearl dropped her head on her husband's shoulders. The Debonair boys were still holding hands as their mother instructed them earlier and they gazing the fire in absolute silence. Ms. Fancy pulled on her daddy's jacket. Otis Jr. looked down at Fancy and asked, "What is it baby?" Fancy said, "Everything will be alright daddy."